HUMMERS
hummingbirds of north america

by
millie miller
and
cyndi nelson

Johnson Books
Boulder

Glimmers of the Past

You are sitting quietly by a forest stream. A brilliant hummingbird darts to a red trumpet flower, hovers a moment & then disappears. The hummer, a true wonder of nature, gets its name from the humming sound of its rapidly beating wings.

Ancient Mexican names likened them to "rays of the sun," the Creoles called them "murmures" & they were known to the Portuguese as "flower kissers."

Although hummingbirds are found only in North & South America, these magical, glittering birds have forever captured people's imagination. Ancient Aztecs wore floor-length ceremonial cloaks made of hummingbird plumage. In the early 1800s, thousands of dried hummingbird skins were shipped to Europe to decorate hats & jewelry. There are some places in Mexico today where they are still dried & sold to people who believe that hummingbirds possess magical powers of love...

and maybe they do as the fascination with hummingbirds continues to flourish.

Millie

✻ Bahama Woodstar

Tidbits

Hummingbirds are mostly tropical and thus prefer the lush vegetation and high humidity of the equatorial belt. The hummingbird family (Trochilidae) consists of an estimated 338 species. Over half of these species can be found in the South American countries of Equador, Columbia, and Brazil alone. Hummers may be small, but they certainly are not wimpy. Some are highly specialized and can thrive up to the 15,000' altitudes and freezing nights of the towering Andean peaks. Others are adapted to the more arid canyons and deserts of Mexico and the southern United States.

Millie

*Rufous-tailed

In this little book, we will be covering the 16 species of hummingbirds that gracefully dart within the United States boundaries (including Alaska)... a mere handfull of hummers. There have also been sightings of "accidental" species north of Old Mexico, drawings of which will be included as these hummers may become more common north of the border with time.

*Accidentals

Giant Hummingbird

Even Big is Little...

Bee Hummingbird

...When Sizing up a Hummer

A Cuban hummer, the Bee hummingbird (Calypte helena) is the tiniest bird in the world, measuring only 2¼" long & weighing 1/15 of an ounce. The largest hummer is the Giant Hummingbird (Patagona gigas) which comes from the Andes & is 8½" long & weighs about ⅗ ounce.

North American hummers come in one basic compact style compared to their ornately feathered southern cousins.

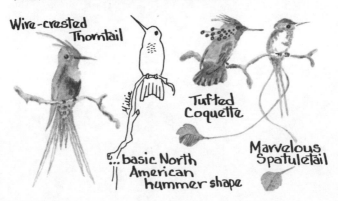

Wire-crested Thorntail

...basic North American hummer shape

Tufted Coquette

Marvelous Spatuletail

Flashy Feathers

As with many other birds, male hummers have the most brilliant costumes. Female feathers are generally duller & in some cases, it's even hard to tell females of one species from another.

Hummingbird feathers have two very different ways of producing color. One is through the actual pigment of the feather & the other is what is called "structural color", the iridescence reflecting off the facets of the feather itself. This reflective feature is what causes a hummer's gorget (throat area) to glitter when you are looking at the bird head on & to become duller when seeing the same bird from another angle. Curiously, the pigment of hummingbird feathers does not include red or yellow.

* Green
Violet-ear

The brilliance & elegance of hummingbird plumage so resembles precious gems that their homes in zoos worldwide are called jewel rooms.

Hummer Dynamics

Hummers have an incredibly high energy output, requiring half of their weight in sugar daily. It has been estimated that a man, who normally eats about 2½ lbs. of food a day, would have to eat more than double his weight in potatoes daily to keep up with a hummer.

A hummingbird's daytime temperature is about 105°F, usually dropping to near 70°F at night. Their resting heartbeat (about 500 beats/minute) more than doubles when excited.

They have a highly efficient respiratory system which includes 9 internal air sacs connected to their lungs by tubes. These air sacs, along with panting, help keep them cool. A quiet hummer breathes about 250 breaths/minute, 10 times greater than that of a pigeon.

* Cuban Emerald

Designed to insert into tubular flowers, hummer bills are usually long, straight & dull black (although a few are reddish or slightly curved). Until recently hummers were thought to suck nectar. Actually, it has been found that their extremely long tongues lick the nectar (approximately 13 licks per second) as capillary action draws it into the tongue.

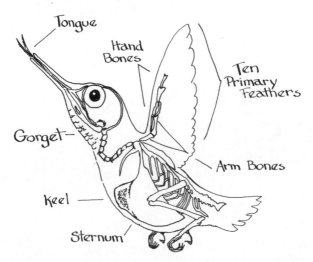

Tongue

Hand Bones

Ten Primary Feathers

Gorget

Arm Bones

Keel

Sternum

Hummers can perform extraordinary aerobatics because of their unique anatomy. Most hummingbird bones are porous, but some, like their wing & leg bones, are hollow. A keel-shaped sternum allows greater area for the attachment of huge flight muscles. Extremely long "hand bones" support the large primary feathers & enable rapid wing strokes while preventing the wings from bending. In a sense, they almost fly with their hands.

Suspended Animation

A hummingbird's lifestyle is always "on the edge"...a dangerous place to be if food supplies are short, health is impaired, and/or there is prolonged bad weather.

Hummers have no down feathers to keep them warm even though they do have more feathers for their surface area than larger birds. However, they do have some ways of conserving energy; most dramatic is a condition called torpidity.

Bumblebee

*

Two hummers can be perched on the same branch...

Hummingbird

The birds fluff out their feathers to allow excess heat to escape, rapidly lowering body temperature & metabolic rate. This hypothermic state is a last resort to stay alive during all or part of a cold night.

one can go torpid & the other does not, depending on their health & energy reserves. Some might avoid torpidity by eating a bigger dinner to have more fuel for the night. Molting birds are more likely to become torpid. Incubating females & fledglings do not go torpid as a fall in temperature would greatly inhibit developing embryos & young.

Torpid hummers appear dead & frozen to the perch, obviously exposing themselves to the dangers of predators since torpidity is a defenseless state. They cannot fly, cry out, or function normally. Breathing can actually stop for short periods of time. It can take over an hour for some birds to waken from the torpid state, their temperatures rising about a degree a minute. In regions where nighttime temperatures go below freezing, hummers must seek some kind of shelter in order to conserve every bit of heat possible.

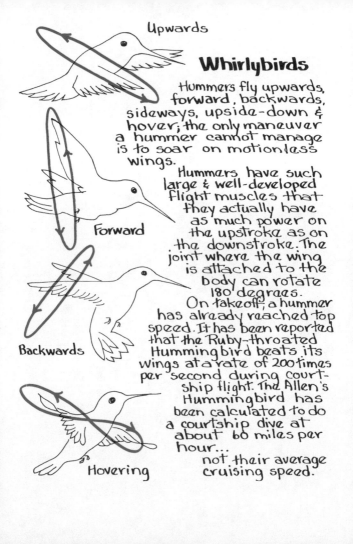

Upwards

Forward

Backwards

Hovering

Whirlybirds

Hummers fly upwards, forward, backwards, sideways, upside-down & hover; the only maneuver a hummer cannot manage is to soar on motionless wings.

Hummers have such large & well-developed flight muscles that they actually have as much power on the upstroke as on the downstroke. The joint where the wing is attached to the body can rotate 180 degrees.

On takeoff, a hummer has already reached top speed. It has been reported that the Ruby-throated Hummingbird beats its wings at a rate of 200 times per second during courtship flight. The Allen's Hummingbird has been calculated to do a courtship dive at about 60 miles per hour...

not their average cruising speed.

Hustling

The courtship of hummingbirds usually begins in spring. After the female has her nest started, she goes out to look for a mate. She's attracted by both the male bird's enticing courtship displays & the amount of food he has to offer in his territory. After she has found a dapper Don Juan to fertilize her eggs, the male returns to being an eligible bachelor & she is left a single parent.

Aerial displays are twofold...mainly to protect the male's territory & also to attract females. Courtship flights are often fast & fancy...spectacular swoops, climbs, dives & intricate patterns in combination with specific vocalizations. The male performs his acrobatics facing the sun, thus showing off his brilliant plumage to the watching female (or territorial intruder).

The Anna's Hummer has one of the most dramatic displays... climbing up as high as 150', continuously watching his audience & sometimes singing momentarily at the peak. The grand finale is a screaming downward dive at top speed, a sensational swoop over his spectator & an explosive popping sound. He may do this up to a dozen times with the metallic popping (thought to be made by his tail feathers) heard up to several hundred feet away.

A more common mating display is the shuttle flight. Frequently done in heavy undergrowth, the male swings back & forth in front of the female... hopefully followed by a chase & copulation.

Each hummer species has a distinct aerial display used by both males & females to protect their homes.

Females may occasionally choose a mate of another species, resulting in hybrid hummers.

Secret Hideaways

Finding a humming-bird's nest is a lot like a treasure hunt.

The first clue is to follow the flight of a female hummer, watching for her most frequented hideaway. These shelters are often found on the forks of tree branches...

...also on cactus, hanging from ledges, clinging to rocks, or suspended from foliage.

The second clue is to look for a cup or cone shaped nest about 2" across, its exterior most often decorated with bits of lichen or bark. Downy feathers, moss, lichens, leaves & soft plant materials line the inside of this little home, usually glued together with spider webs (which also secure the nest to its base). Some species nesting in colder climates build with thicker insulation.

The nest is shaped by the expectant mom, knitting in new materials with her bill & pushing her breast against the outside of the nest to give it a cup-like shape. Jogging in place, she compacts the downy fluff on the inside of the cup. The upper edge curves inward to form a tight seal with her body. Strong & waterproof, nests usually take from one day to 2 weeks to build, and the mom may continue to add & decorate after her eggs are laid. Some hummers build new nests every year, others reuse the old or even stack them.

Should this treasure chest be found, the grand prize is to see it filled with 2 miniature white eggs or wee baby hummers.

Jelly Beans

Hummingbirds almost always lay 2 white eggs, each about the size of a jelly bean. These are actually very large compared to the size of the mom, both eggs being from 10 to 20% of her weight. To develop properly, the eggs need to be turned regularly & kept at around 90°F. On cold or rainy days, the mom must fluff out & separate her feathers, sealing her body over the nest to give adequate warmth. On hot days, she may shade the eggs by standing over them.

Baby hummers hatch in about 15 to 22 days, a relatively long time compared to other birds. After the embryo has consumed all the food in the egg, it hatches with the help of 2 specialized features. One, an "egg tooth", is a hardened point on the tip of the undeveloped short bill. The other is a big hatching muscle on the back of its head which gives greater force to the "egg tooth" in pecking out of the shell. Once hatched, these features disappear.

Any broken shells are disposed of by the mother so as not to attract predators. The stouthearted moms fearlessly protect their nests, driving off enemies much larger than themselves... even hawks & snakes.

Tiny Boppers

Because nestlings essentially have no feathers, are blind & have only tiny bills, they need constant care. From birth, whenever they hear their mom's wings or sense movement, they beg for food. Baby food consists of regurgitated nectar & insects, skillfully poked down their throats by mom. A hummingbird's nest is always tidy... nestlings will do acrobatics to toilet train over the side.

Within 8-12 days after hatching, the nestlings have grown enough pinfeathers to maintain their own body temperature. As the days go by, the nest is usually flexible enough to accomodate the growing hummers.

After a few days of exercising & fluttering their wings in the nest, their first flight is usually successful. Landings may take more practice. The nest is deserted when the fledglings leave home in about 21 days. After this, some moms may still preen & feed their youngsters until they are completely self-sufficient. Unless the mom leaves the territory first, she will eventually shoo her fledglings away to their own independence.

A lucky hummer may live about ten years.

Bouquets and Bugs

Hummingbirds cannot live on nectar alone. They devour a fair number of insects as well, nibbling them from the inside of flowers, around plants and trees, nabbing them in midair, or even stealing them from spider webs.

* Plain-capped Starthroat

cyndi

Their long bills are especially adapted for extracting the nectar found at the base of the corollas of flowers. The flowers frequented by hummers are usually red or reddish, but they will try any color. The sugar concentration is more critical than color. Hummingbird flowers are generally tubular, odorless, open during the day, often have a longer blooming time & frequently have no perch. Hummers feed 5 to 8 times per hour, assimilating almost 100% of the sugar, gaining weight as the day goes on in preparation for the cooler night. Often they will hover while drinking, although they might prefer to conserve energy on a perch. They drink water in addition to nectar.

Although hummers may dine on a variety of flowers, their eating habits are critical to certain flowers. While feeding, they collect pollen on their heads & upon visiting another flower, cross pollinate. A few flowers have evolved specifically for the hummingbird & these flowers are not visited by bees.

How Sweet it is...

Hummingbirds like "fast food" & a hummingbird feeder can be a quick & easy way to attract them into your territory. Early in the spring, fill the feeder with... 1 part white sugar dissolved in 4 to 5 parts red water. If the feeder is red already, the color of the water is not important. Also, hummers might appreciate a feeder with a perch. **NO HONEY!**

It is also possible to plant your garden to attract hummingbirds. There are certain flowers they prefer, usually reddish in color & generally tubular. Most of these blooms are horizontal or hanging & are arranged so that there is unentangling space around them. Some ideas for common flowers to plant in a garden are:

Beard Tongues
Century Plants
Indian Paintbrush
Trumpet Vines
Penstamon
Buckeye
Columbine
Locoweed
Larkspur
Monkey Flower
Scarlet Lobelia
Morning-glory
Honeysuckle
Indian Pink
Bee-balm
Ocotillo
Fuchsia
Thistles
Currents
Gilia

Use your imagination for more ideas or contact your local nursery. Then sit back & enjoy!

The Hedgehog Cactus is fertilized only by hummers.

Millie

CHARACTERISTICS...
3⅓" long. Male has metallic
green crown & fiery red-orange gorget.
White chest & greenish back (Rufous hummer
has distinct rufous back). Sides, rump & tail rufous.
Underparts are cinnamon.
Females hard to distinguish
from Rufous females.
HABITAT... California coastal
mountain meadows, brushy canyons, redwood forest
edges & city gardens.
TIDBITS... Typical pendulum
courtship display has dive clocked up to 60 mph.
Moss covered nests have a
greenish cast.

Allen's   Selasphorus sasin

HABITAT...
Homes in chaparral, edges of redwood forests, mountains up to 6,000 feet, live oak trees & backyard gardens.

CHARACTERISTICS... 3½-4" long.
Male's whole head & gorget is a brilliant rose-red except for a white spot behind the eye. Back is green & underparts are grayish. No rufous coloring.

Female's gray & green parts are darker than male. She is not a redhead, having only a splash of red on her throat. Similar but larger than Costa female and rounder than Black-chinned.

TIDBITS... Doesn't truly migrate but resides mostly in California. Occasionally vacations in S. Arizona. Un-hummer-like, breeds in winter & early spring. Feeds heavily on insects. Prefers red gooseberries.

The largest hummer in California and the only one that sings. Has squeaky warbling song from perch and a chattering "chick" note while feeding.

Calypte anna

Anna's

Millie

CHARACTERISTICS... 3½" long. Male has bright
green hood, throat & chest. Upper back is
also green, becoming chestnut colored
ending in purple tail feathers. Rufous-
chestnut coloration in the wings. Grayish-
brown underparts. The bill is black on top
& reddish underneath.

Female is very similar to the male but is
duller with less green extending down
abdomen. Her bill is also black & red.

HABITAT... Mountain streams,
edges of high forests and
pine-oak woodlands.

TIDBITS... This little green monk prefers
the banana plantations of old Mexico
but does nest north of the border
in SE Arizona.

Male sings
a loud
"bob-o-leak"
song.

Amazilia
beryllina

Berylline

CHARACTERISTICS... 3¼ - 3¾" long. Male has a black head & chin with a white spot behind the eyes. Wears a gleaming violet band above a white collar & chest. Back is green. Tail slightly forked & purplish-bronze. Underside is gray.

Female is basically green with white underparts. She has a metallic green-gray tail, the outer 3 feathers white tipped and the lower center feathers black. Very similar to female Anna's and Costa's... but thinner.

TIDBITS... Courtship display is usually a pendulum pattern. Listen for a low "tup" call & the dry buzz of wings in flight. Nests look like wooly yellowish cups.

HABITAT... Frequents canyons, semi-arid country near water, chaparral & suburbs.

Chief pollinator of Chuparosa.

Archilochus alexandri

Black-chinned

CHARACTERISTICS...
   4½ - 5¼" long.
Male has gray-green
crown with white stripes
above & below eyes.
   Brilliant colbalt blue   gorget and
brownish-gray breast with slate underparts. Long blue-black tail has distinct
white tips on outer three feathers.
Female similar but with brownish-green throat.

HABITAT... Wooded mountain canyons in lush
streamside
   vegetation.
                    TIDBITS... Largest resident
                       hummer in U.S. Rapid &
                       aggressive fliers often
                  fanning their tail feathers to
             show off their white spots. A
          heavy insect eater, especially when
          nectar supply is low. Female
          builds nest under natural or
          manmade "roofs", usually
          near water. Apt to return to
          same nest yearly. Often
          raises more than one brood a
     season. When perched or in flight, makes
   a regular "seep" noise.

   Lampornis clemenciae
   Blue-throated

CHARACTERISTICS... 3¼-4" long. Male has dark green crown with small white spot behind the eye. Back also green extending into a forked dark steel blue tail. Flashy green-blue sequined gorget, breast & sides.

Lower abdomen is white.

Bill is red with a black tip.

Female similar but, as usual, duller with grayish underside and bronze-green tail.

HABITAT... Arid country & rocky canyons where mesquite and agave are found.

TIDBITS...
May look black from a distance. Often dines on insects. Similar to White-eared hummer, which has long white stripe behind the eyes. Nests in southern Arizona. Sound made during courtship has been likened to the zing of a rifle bullet.

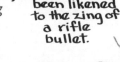

Cynanthus latirostris

Broad-billed

CHARACTERISTICS... 4-4½" long. Male has green crown, back & upper tail. Rounded tail & rosy-red gorget distinguish it from the ruby-red gorget & forked tail of the Ruby-throated Hummer. White chest & grey underparts.

Female similar to female Rufous & Allen's. Also like female Calliope but larger.

HABITAT... Mountain woodlands, willow thickets, and meadows. Also city gardens.

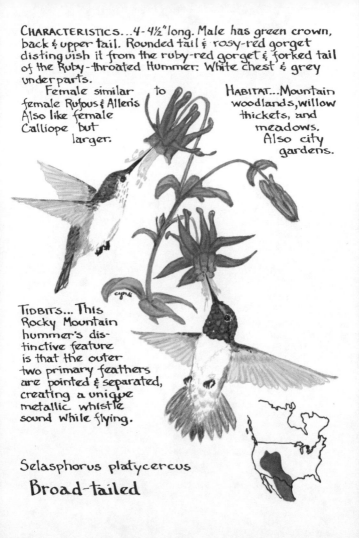

TIDBITS... This Rocky Mountain hummer's distinctive feature is that the outer two primary feathers are pointed & separated, creating a unique metallic whistle sound while flying.

Selasphorus platycercus
Broad-tailed

CHARACTERISTICS... 4-4½" long. Males & females alike with green crown & back. Throat & upper breast iridescent green. Lower breast & belly cinnamon-buff. Rufous tail is slightly forked with chestnut-colored tips.

Red-orange bill with black tip.

HABITAT... Dense thickets, scrubby growth in semi-arid woods, creeping vines along streams or gullies & citrus groves.

TIDBITS... Nests in Rio Grande Valley of Southern Texas.

This hummer is unusual because of its reddish bill and the similarity of the sexes.

Amazilia yucatanensis

Buff-bellied

CHARACTERISTICS... 2¾"-3½" long. Male has metallic green head and candy-caned striped gorget which flares when excited. Gold-green back & brownish tail feathers. Cinnamon-gray underparts. Female has lightly speckled throat. Resembles Rufous, Black-chinned and Broad-tailed females but is smaller.

HABITAT... likes conifer forests & open grasslands in high elevations.

TIDBITS... Smallest bird in North America. Nests closely resemble pinecones or mistletoe knots.

Arches tail feathers up while hovering.

Makes "chip" & squeaking noise while feeding.

Stellula calliope

Calliope

CHARACTERISTICS... 3-3½" long. Male has a violet-purple crown & a matching gorget with unique, conspicuous side feathers. He has a green back & darker green tail. Underside is gray-green.

Female hard to distinguish from the Black-chinned & Anna female except for the light purplish spots on her throat.

TIDBITS... Partial to insects and red flowers, especially red beardtongue. Characteristically flies an arc pattern between flower clusters.

Has a "chick" call ending in a whistle.

Able to go through breeding season without water.

HABITAT... Prefers hot deserts and arid terrain... especially near ocotillo, mesquites, sages, yuccas & cholla cacti.

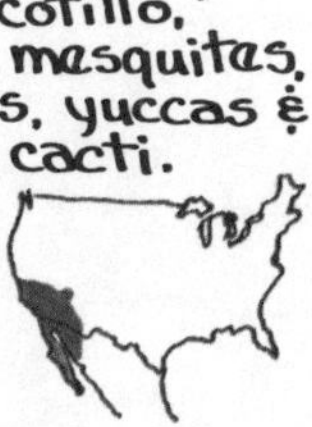

Calypte costae
Costa's

Millie

CHARACTERISTICS... 3¾" long. Male has green crown. Brilliant violet-purple gorget has elongated side feathers similar to Costa's. Back is green extending into a greenish-brown, noticeably forked tail. Rufous-colored patches on the sides & grayish underparts. Decurved black bill.

Female is similar to male but with buff-colored underparts & rounded tail.

HABITAT... Open deserts with favored agaves...also mountain slopes up to 18,000 ft.

cyndi

TIDBITS... Commonly nests in Southwestern Texas in the Chisos Mountains. Often dines on spiders and insects taken from webs or flowers. The only North American hummingbird with a decurved bill. Has a piercing shriek when defending territory.

Calothorax lucifer

Lucifer

cyndi

CHARACTERISTICS... 4½-5" long. Male has
iridescent purple crown & striking
white spot behind eyes. Metallic
green gorget with velvety black breast.
Green back. Slightly forked tail feathers
with grey tips.
Female has green head & back.
Speckled throat & grey underparts have scale-
like appearance. Grey tips on corner feathers of
square tail.

HABITAT...
Mountain woods
of the Southwest.

TIDBITS...Appears black
from a distance. Flies more
slowly than other hummers.
Especially fond of insects &
attracted to agaves because of their abundant
insect life. Occasionally spotted in
Colorado mountains.

Eugenes fulgens
Magnificent (Rivoli's)

CHARACTERISTICS... 3-4" long. Male has a radiant ruby gorget. Head has green crown, is black on the sides & has a tiny white spot behind the eyes. Back is metallic green. Has distinctively forked brownish-black tail.

Underside is whitish-gray.

Female is similar but has dull white throat & a white tipped rounded tail.

HABITAT... Backyard gardens, forests & parks. Often found hanging around sapsucker holes.

TIDBITS... The only Hummer found east of the Mississippi.

Although one of the smallest of all hummers, it stores up enough fat to successfully make a non-stop, 500 mile migration across the Gulf of Mexico. Listen for their squeaking voice as they fly.

Fond of Nasturtiums & Bee-balm.

Archilochus colubris

Ruby-throated

CHARACTERISTICS... 3-4" long. Male has bronze-green crown & polished copper-red gorget above white breast. Only North American hummer with total rufous back (distinguishing it from the Allen's rufous-green back). Rufous-buff underparts & dark tipped rufous tail.

Female has green head & back, speckled throat, rufous sides and underparts. Very similar to Allen's & Broad-tailed females.

HABITAT... Prefer chaparral, mountain meadows & forests up to timberline but also enjoy anything from the seacoast to urban gardens.

TIDBITS... Summers farther north (Alaska and Yukon) than any American hummer.

Both sexes extremely ferocious in defending their territories, readily attacking other hummingbirds & huge predators.

Selasphorus rufous

Rufous

CHARACTERISTICS...3¾-4¼" long. Male has striking violet-blue crown. Back, sides & tail dull bronze-green. Entire underparts snowy white. Bright red bill with a black tip.

Female similar to male but has a duller crown.

HABITAT...
Canyons, along streambanks, scrub oak, and deserts.

TIDBITS...
This aggressive and easy to identify hummer (the only one without a brilliant gorget) is found most often in Mexico but nests in S.W. New Mexico & S.E. Arizona.

Amazilia violiceps

Violet-crowned

CHARACTERISTICS... 3½" long. Male has a violet crown and chin with brilliant emerald-green gorget. Definite white stripe behind the eyes.
Back is greenish-gold, ending with a square tipped, rusty tail. His sides are greenish with white underparts. Bill is red with a black tip.

Female is similar to male but has green speckled throat.

HABITAT...
Woodlands near streams & scrubby undergrowth, especially of oak forests.

TIDBITS... Males make a tinkling sound when perched. They sometimes gather into small groups to sing.

Nest in S.E. Arizona. Females have been observed caring for two broods at a time or raising an orphaned family along with their own.

Hylocharis leucotis
White-eared

Hummingbird Moth
(Sphinx or Hawk Moth)

Often mistaken for hummers because they can fly at high speeds, hover and suck nectar from flowers. When at rest, a body length tongue coils under their heads.

Dedication...
   to my Mom & Dad whose love and generosity equal the hummingbird's amazing beauty and flight.
                    Cyndi

references...

Johnsgard, Paul A. <u>The Hummingbirds of North America</u>. Washington, D.C.: Smithsonian Institution Press, 1983.

Skutch, Alexander F. <u>The Life of the Hummingbird</u>. New York: Crown Publishers, Inc. 1973.

Terres, John K. <u>Audubon Society Encyclopedia of North American Birds</u>. New York: Alfred A. Knopf, Inc. 1980.

Tyrrell, Esther Quesada & Robert A. <u>Hummingbirds: Their Life & Behavior</u>. New York: Crown Publishers, Inc. 1985.

Udvardy, Miklos, D.F. <u>The Audubon Society Field Guide to North American Birds: Western Region</u>. New York: Alfred A. Knopf, Inc., 1977.

Wetmore, Alexander. <u>Song and Garden Birds of North America</u>. Washington, D.C.: National Geographic Society, 1964.

Victoria & Albert

Pussy cat, pussy cat,
    Where have you been?
I've been to London
    To look at the Queen.
Pussy cat, pussy cat,
    What did you there?
I frightened a little mouse
    Under her chair.